Launch

Launch

A Guide For The Season Of Lent

Richard P. Zimmerman

LAUNCH
A Guide For The Season of Lent
Novo Civitas Books and Resources
novocivitas.com

Novo Civitas

Books & Resources

Copyright © 2019 by Richard P. Zimmerman

All rights reserved. No part of this book may be reproduced in any form without the written permission of the author, with the exception of brief excerpts for the purpose of review or to publicize group gatherings for those who are using this book for group study.

Scripture quotations taken from The Holy Bible, New International Version,® NIV.® Copyright © 1973, 1978, 1984, 2011 by Biblica, Inc.® Used by permission. All rights reserved worldwide.

PAPERBACK ISBN 978-0-578-60628-6
EBOOK ISBN 978-0-578-60629-3

A ship in harbor is safe, but that is not what ships are built for.
—J. A. Shedd.

Contents

1. Before Beginning — 1
2. Lent Is For Launching — 9
3. Put It Into Practice — 21
4. Ash Wednesday — 37
5. First Week of Lent: The Wedge — 43
6. Second Week of Lent: Leaving Your City Behind — 51
7. Third Week of Lent: Comparison — 57
8. Fourth Week of Lent: Emptiness — 67
9. Fifth Week of Lent: Knowing Hope — 75
10. Holy Week: Make The Most Of These Eight Days — 83
11. Easter And Beyond — 89
12. A Word After Launch — 95

In Gratitude

1

Before Beginning

He has saved us and called us to a holy life—not because of anything we have done but because of his own purpose and grace. This grace was given us in Christ Jesus before the beginning of time, but it has now been revealed through the appearing of our Savior, Christ Jesus, who has destroyed death and has brought life and immortality to light through the gospel.

II Timothy 1:9-10

Before Beginning

Many people have heard of the idea of giving up something for Lent and they are intrigued. For others the fast of Lent, or foregoing some pleasure, is a regular part of Lent every year. It can feel good to have a concrete challenge, a sacrifice in order to reassure myself that I am really engaged–that I am really trying.

But it may not be so helpful to quickly dive in to that kind of a spiritual discipline. We all have unique personalities with our own individual challenges. Is it really best for everyone to simply think up something to give up for several weeks? Some people may need to add something to their daily routine rather than taking something away. For many different reasons, sacrifice is not always the best path to spiritual growth. While sacrifice is sometimes effective as a way of cooperating with the Holy Spirit in your own growth, it can lead to pride, it sometimes fosters resentment towards God, and it may be a distraction from what God is intending to do with the next season of spiritual growth in your life.

Instead of thinking

> **Do you need a prayer partner for this study?**
>
> Consider asking a friend to go through the study with you. While this will certainly work as a personal study, you may find it more helpful if you have the support and accountability of a prayer partner.

LAUNCH

of Lent as a time of sacrifice, what if you imagine this as a season of setting aside lesser things in order to launch a renewed sense of the adventure of following the resurrected Christ?

The readings and reflection questions in this book are designed to help you take a lingering look at the things that can hold people back from launching into the adventure of following Jesus on a quest of life at its fullest.

To begin, read over some of the brief suggestions and ideas for adding a spiritual growth practice during Lent. These are not elaborate, difficult, or onerous. They are simple daily practices you may choose to do throughout Lent as a way of growing closer to God and more peaceful and effective in your daily living. Then each week you will read about a topic that will help support you in this journey.

This study does ask for a fairly high level of commitment. I hope you will find this to be a refreshing challenge. The stories, thoughts, questions, Bible references, and suggestions are all intended to help you see God's work in your life and take steps to launch into new patterns of faithfulness. Many people will not have the time to read every part. Read only what will help you. Each segment is designed to support you as you make choices for how you are going to let this Easter launch you into following Jesus in new ways, or as a way of remembering some of the old ways and taking them up again. So take the parts that help you, and leave the rest behind.

• Spend some time before Ash Wednesday in prayerful assessment of where you are in your spiritual journey.

Before Beginning

- Read the chapters, *Lent Is For Launching*, and *Put It Into Practice*, and consider what one thing God is asking you to work on during Lent this year.

For the Leader of the Group
If you are using this book as a guide for group study

This book is designed to lead people through a time of intentional study, reflection, and action, throughout the season of Lent in preparation for the celebration of Easter. It begins with having the individuals in the small group engage in some reflection a couple of weeks before the beginning of Lent. They will search for a single intentional spiritual discipline to maintain up until Easter. The group members then gather weekly to encourage each other to keep going and to share in a Bible study on a topic supporting spiritual growth.

Read this section if you are leading a group through this study.

The leader will need to be selective in setting a schedule for group meetings. Things will work out best if you take a few moments with a calendar and plan your meeting dates and topics a month or so before Lent begins. Now, if it is already too late for that don't worry. Just a little adjustment will make it all work. The plan in this book includes discussion questions for nine meetings. But the group may not choose to meet on every one of those weeks, so feel free to skip some of the sessions. The studies are not sequential so you can skip a session or two without having to make it up later. And since all group members will have their own book, they can choose to read the sections you skip if they want to. Your church may have an Ash Wednesday service and so you may not want to gather as a group during that week. You could simply skip the Bible study discussion in that chapter. Likewise, most churches have many activities during holy week and so the group may simply skip that Bible study discussion as well.

Skipping sections will not soften the seriousness of this study. The challenging part comes from the seriousness of engaging in an intentional daily spiritual practice for a period of several weeks on end. That is much more important than trying to read every part of the book or participate in every group meeting.

On the other hand, even though you might skip some of the sections in the book, I sincerely hope your group will still gather during the week *after* Easter to conclude this study. Lent is meant to prepare us to receive new power and grace for living as we participate in the resurrection at Easter. So it is important to gather during the week after Easter and reflect on what everyone has learned, even though people are often tired and ready to take a break once Easter is done. The challenge is to stay focused for the season, to let the Spirit work in your group as you aim toward Easter morning when the resurrection is once again planted in your soul, and then to let that reality change the daily lives of your group members in enduring patterns.

Make sure there is a Bible for everyone at the group meetings.

While many passages of scripture are fully printed out in this book, the passages suggested for group study are not. Whether on smart phone, tablet, or with Bible in hand, each person needs to be able to refer to the Bible during the small group discussions.

Before Beginning

For Individuals

Read this section if you are using this as an individual study.

At the very beginning, when I was first creating this study, I was envisioning a daily personal study for Lent. So if you are doing this study on your own, you are actually doing what I originally intended. I tend to be a person who leans toward independent study, so I can relate to your desire to do this on your own. I would suggest acquiring a notebook to use as your journal as you work your way through the sections. Try to discipline yourself to make this a weekly, or even daily habit of progressing through the sections. Where the study calls for group discussion, you could write your answers to the questions.

I hope you will find someone to share with in some way as you undertake this study. Oftentimes spiritual growth becomes more solid when you tell someone else what God is teaching you, and what you are doing in response to what you have learned.

Reading Schedule

For groups and individuals.

Read these chapters in the weeks before Ash Wednesday:

1. Before Beginning
2. Lent Is For Launching
3. Put It Into Practice

Read this chapter before or on Ash Wednesday:

4. Ash Wednesday

LAUNCH

Read each of these chapters during the weeks of Lent. Read "The First Week of Lent" sometime after the First Sunday of Lent, and so on.

5. First Week of Lent: The Wedge
6. Second Week of Lent: Leaving Your City Behind
7. Third Week of Lent: Comparison
8. Fourth Week of Lent: Emptiness
9. Fifth Week of Lent: Knowing Hope
10. Holy Week: Make The Most Of These Eight Days

Read this chapter after Easter:

11. Easter And Beyond

Read this chapter as you wish:

12. A Word After Launch

2

Lent Is For Launching

The end of our lifelong journey and quest is not merely a change of location, as if some celestial moving van could take you and me and our stuff from our current address to a house in the sky. It involves a profound transformation, the emergence of our true self, so that in becoming like Christ we most truly become ourselves—at home in our skin and in our soul, as Irenaeus said, "humans fully alive."

Leighton Ford, *The Attentive Life: Discerning God's Presence in All Things*

Lent Is For Launching

All too often life seems like a roller coaster. It can be thrilling, or even scary, with wild twists and turns, but at the end you are back at the same place you started. We all seem to carry around inside of ourselves a certain kind of death–destructive habits, impenetrable barriers, debilitating tendencies, or flaws in how we relate to those around us. These things make some relationships seem impossible and get in the way of how we relate to God.

And yet what we really want is life at it fullest. We want to be free. We want to be strong and wise. We want to contribute to the beauty of life on this planet. We want to be close to our Creator, hiding nothing from his watchful care.

It is like the picture on the cover of this book. Imagine yourself on the shore of a beautiful ocean or lake. The weather is perfect and the gentle waves assure you that the boat would be gently cradled on calm waters if you took it out. But the boat is sunk and grounded. No oars are in sight. A mooring line holds the boat in place. If you are going to launch that boat you will need to do some work.

The same is true of the spiritual life of most people. We want a closer relationship with God. We wish we were more effective for his kingdom. We want more peaceful and intimate relationships with our closest friends and family. We want to be free of debilitating habits. We want to be done with anxiety and fear. What must be done to make those things happen?

From the earliest times Christians have used the fasting season of Lent as a means of spiritual growth. Fasting is a way of weakening the grip our bodies have over our spirits. It prepares us for deeper prayer and meditation, and it is a way of presenting our repentance before God.

So how does all of that prepare us so that Easter has the effect of launching us into the new life promised to us? On an immediate level, fasting means abstaining from food. On a temporary basis, for a definite reason, we voluntarily give up one of God's good gifts in order to grow. This could mean completely going without food for a time, it could mean eating more basic food for a set period, or it could simply mean reducing the amount we eat during a season.

Americans are so diet-conscious that weight loss always looms in the background when food is considered. But we should make a conscious effort to keep the motivations centered on spiritual growth rather than on personal improvement goals.

How Long Is Lent?

Lent goes from Ash Wednesday up to the Saturday before Easter. This pattern recalls the 40 days Jesus spent fasting in the wilderness in preparation for the beginning of his mission. But if you count each day from Ash Wednesday through the Saturday before Easter you get 46. So how is it 40 days?

Since every Sunday is a celebration of the resurrection, the Sundays of Lent are not part of the fast.

Since fasting is a matter of the heart and is all about spiritual growth, my thinking immediately moves beyond food. Consider what other ways you might use the season of Lent as a time of preparation for growth into new areas. This may require you to assess your state of stagnation and choose to get back out onto the unknown waters in search of the way life was meant to be. So the plan to take on a specific practice for Lent involves an assessment of those things that are holding you back. This requires honesty about the ways you may have chosen to quietly settle into compromises for the sake of creating an illusion of peace.

> **Fasting In Scripture**
>
> Jeremiah 36:9
> Joel 1:14
> Matthew 6:16-18

Launching out onto the waters of God's plan for our lives means living like Jesus in concrete ways. The gospels narrate the ministry of Jesus as a journey undertaken for the sake of completing the mission given to him by his Father. Jesus left his home in Nazareth and headed out into his world in search of hurting and lost people. But more than that, he was always on a road that would wind around through several different places and yet inevitably end at the cross. And the most frequent invitation given to those who want to be near him was, "Follow me."

The implications are obvious. The most fundamental way to conceive of life as a follower of Jesus is to think of yourself as a person launched out on a spiritual quest in search of where Jesus is going in the world. So while Lent may involve some form of fasting, our eyes should be firmly fixed on how the fast makes us more ready to live fully in the challenge to follow Jesus.

LAUNCH

This can, of course, be done while never leaving home or physically traveling anywhere. At some level the journey and voyage images are symbolic. You may be sent on a mission to the very place you were born and your quest may be to follow Jesus along a very lengthy span of time without physically going anywhere at all. But that shouldn't be an excuse for staying static. To be a Christ-follower is to be launched out on an adventure into the unknown, even for those who are called by God to never relocate to any other geographic place.

But let's be honest. Many people who are followers of Jesus are not going anywhere at all–neither physically nor spiritually. Many who have promised to take up their cross daily and follow Jesus have turned that adventure into routine dabbling in the things of faith. In fact, stagnation is so common that it seems inevitable.

For a moment take a lingering look at the things that can hold people back from launching into the adventure of following Jesus on a quest of life at its fullest. Are you bogged down by past mistakes? That is like water sloshing around in the bottom of the boat before it can even be launched. Are the anchors in place? Sometimes we say we want to move forward, but no forward movement is possible with a heavy weight attached. What is really keeping you from traveling by faith wherever Jesus might take you? The purpose of this study is to help you identify the things that hold you back and to discover the courage to launch.

That takes strength. Deep inner strength is the result of preparation. How did Jesus arrive at the moment of his arrest with calm resolve and the strength to carry out the will of his Father? The answer to this question comes in the sequence of events remembered during Lent every year.

40 Days of Resisting Temptation

Follow the events of Jesus's life to find the pattern of deep inner strength. Jesus would gather people to teach them. He was not tied down to the way things are. He was looking toward and living in a world that he could see, but a world invisible to the eye. He was a healer. He had compassion on people, a compassion literally flowing from his hands. No army could achieve the mission of Jesus, so it is more difficult than simply raising an army. Jesus was confronting power with transforming love. That put him on a collision course with people who wouldn't mind killing an innocent man, because to them, power was more important than love.

The strength of Jesus arose from a vision of who was truly fighting this battle. He didn't try to use power to conquer the forces arrayed against him. He didn't coerce

Supporting Actions

Pause and consider the things you do daily to encourage consistent spiritual growth. These are things that support growth and help you stick with your commitments. For example, a person choosing to fast for a time will find the fasting more effective if it is supported by actions like:
- a commitment to daily personal prayer.
- Bible reading
- a journal to regularly write about one struggle that you seem to always face, or one consolation that lifts you.
- service to others

Which of these actions are a regular part of your life?
Which are things that you have done in the past?
Which of these are new to you?

people to become pawns in his plans. Jesus lived always in the intersecting reality of the unseen power at work in him. He turned away from things of lesser importance and calmly embraced the reality of his Father's power. And the disciples saw it. Experiencing first hand the life of Jesus sent the disciples on a lifelong quest of living in the power of his transforming love.

The strength to live this way flowed, in part, from the strength gained through preparation. Jesus was led by the Spirit into the wilderness. He fasted for forty days and confronted the core temptations that represented the main challenges he would face.

It is my hope that your journey through these weeks will have the same effect on you and you will launch out into life at its fullest in a lifelong journey of truly following Jesus. In the next chapter I provide an extensive description of several different ways that people typically get stuck, along with suggestions for how this season of Lent could be a time for growing beyond those problems. Following that chapter, the readings for each week of Lent are arranged around some of the central themes necessary for launching a spiritual journey.

About Lent

Lent is a season of spiritual preparation for Easter. It is usually a time of reflection on the temptations and sufferings of Christ. Many people take Lent as a time for fasting and repentance in order to be ready to fully embrace the joy and celebration of Easter.

Lent goes back to the time just a couple of hundred years after the life of Jesus. Some people think of Lent as a Catholic or Orthodox thing, but actually Lent is practiced in many different ways throughout many kinds of churches. In the Eastern Orthodox and Roman Catholic churches Lent is a season of fasting. The church prescribes this fasting and obedience to the fast is part of being a practicing Christian for them. The aim is to simplify life for a season in order to be able to focus on deeper matters. Beyond fasting, many seek to add some new practices that will help them to become more like Christ.

Let God use the season of Lent to prepare you for launching into the next year of your resurrection faith.

For Personal Reflection

Spend a few moments considering the present state of your life before moving on from this chapter. On the next page I have created a diagram of spiritual life. Moving from left to right represents the passing of time, so that the far left is your birth and the future is to the right. On the diagram I have entered some arrows and labels describing some possible seasons of growth, decline, or stagnation. Consider if any of these are fitting descriptions of your current state. You might circle one line and description if it best describes you right now. If none of these are quite right to describe you, what would? You might take your own sheet of paper and make a diagram of your own life that adequately assesses your recent journey, or you may even want to diagram your whole life in this way, charting the ups and downs.

Notice this is not a diagram of how you felt at various points in your life, or when people around you thought things were going well. It is not a success chart. It is meant to identify times when God was helping you to grow spiritually. If you are wondering to yourself *what really is spiritual growth?* then you are asking the right question. Take some time to consider that question and talk to others if you don't have answers.

Once you have made the diagram, take some time to consider where you are right now, and what factors of your own choosing, or forces from the world around you, are shaping the vitality of your life.

LAUNCH

Diagram of my life

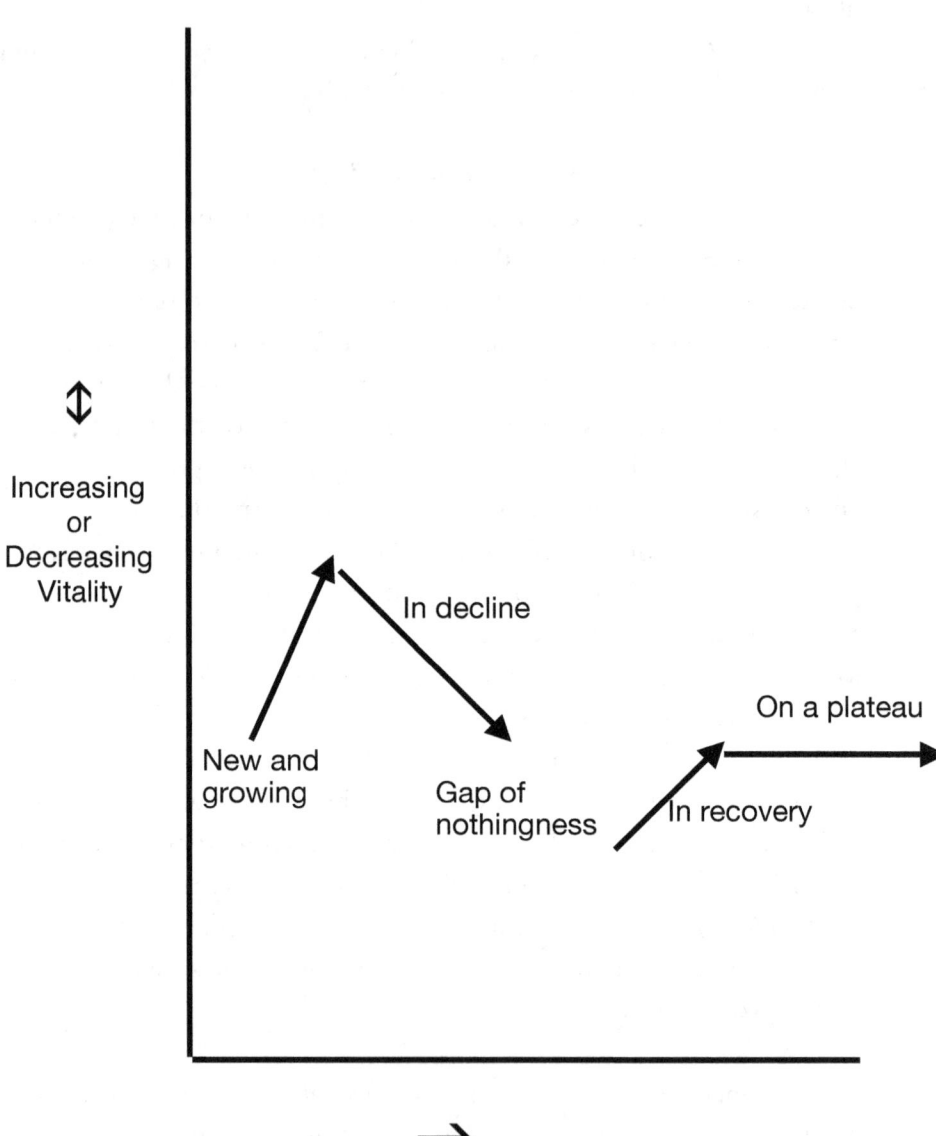

18

Questions to Consider

What does the diagram suggest to you about your spiritual vitality over time?

What steps have you taken in the past that helped you grow closer to God?

Do you find yourself longing for something that is missing?

What is it, and what might you put into practice to help it return?

3

Put It Into Practice

Whatever you have learned or received or heard from me, or seen in me—put it into practice. And the God of peace will be with you.

The Apostle Paul, Philippians 4:9

Put It Into Practice

We spend a lot of our lives dreaming about the good life, wishing we had everything and wishing life would be easy. But having everything we could possibly want is not always so good for us. In fact it actually could be toxic. So when Lent comes around it is common to give up things for the season in order to grow spiritually. Maybe it is giving up something like chocolate. And yet sometimes people who give up chocolate for Lent become more obsessed with chocolate before, during, and after Lent, even as they are trying to go without it. The spiritual practice of abstaining from a pleasure sometimes works in reverse.

Can I really

> ## Read this chapter before Ash Wednesday.

> ## The Plan
>
> This week you will consider the challenge to take on a spiritual practice for Lent. Read this section and consider how God might be leading you to grow in this season of preparation for Easter.

do anything about the niggling little sins and nagging barriers that hold me back in life? Or will growth always be painful, haphazard, disappointing, and subject to frequent regressions? Through the season of Lent, and by the power released in Easter, can our lives be changed for the better?

Yes. Though we all struggle, Lent is a time to prepare for launch—a time to get started on a journey—a time to shake off the mooring lines of the past—a time to prepare for living in the power of our faith. Easter should be a day of launching. So the spiritual practices of Lent are designed to propel you toward growth in peace and effectiveness in truly loving people. This may require assessing your state of stagnation and choosing to get back out onto unknown waters of a search of the way life was meant to be. That requires honesty about the ways we have chosen to quietly settle into compromises for the sake of creating an illusion of peace.

But where do *you* begin this Lenten journey as you prepare for launching into God's plans for your life? What burned out dreams need to die? Where are you trapped in the past? How much do you expect from God? Or are you done with expecting anything from God?

> Lent is most effective if you choose just one small practice to add to your life during the season.

Once you have a general idea of where God is leading you in this season, consider what form your journey might take. What is one thing you might commit to doing daily throughout these days?

As you consider what one spiritual practice you might choose to put in place for Lent, here are some scripture passages, some questions, and some and thoughts that might spark an idea. But be certain not to get distracted by the many possibilities. Lent is most effective if you choose just one small thing—one thought to dwell on, one prayer to repeat, one intentional action, one bad habit to release, or one good habit to add. The following suggestions are meant to help you choose what works for you this year, but this will work best if you are motivated to follow your own plan throughout the entire season of Lent.

- **Against the Wind Philippians 4:10-13**

    Consider what forces push against you in your quest to follow Jesus. Do fear, anxiety, or discouragement get in your way? Remember that you are not expected to float along placidly in this world. What obstacles are in your way? What causes you to lose focus? Where do you find energy to keep going? What circumstance is getting the best of you?

Suggested Spiritual Practice

Once you identify what is working against you, find a daily practice that will turn your attention to the power of God, and away from the discouraging circumstance. For example, every day you might say to yourself, "I am discouraged by (whatever it is), but I can be content in this situation. I can do this through Christ because he strengthens me."

- **Where Are You Starting? Where Are You Going?**

    Our lives are spent in the in-between. The final goal, the destination, the whole point of what God has been doing with humanity lies ahead. The story of the Bible is a journey by people of faith out of a land of hopelessness toward God's good vision for us.

LAUNCH

Along the way it helps to pause and consider where you have come from, where you are right now, and where you are going. Lent might be a time of praying about God's direction for your life.

Suggested Spiritual Practice

Try "journaling the journey." Get a notebook and spend a few minutes per day writing about the trajectory of your life. Start with prompts like,

- I felt like I was doing what I am meant to do when . . .

- The one thing I don't want to miss in life is . . .

- **Various Kinds of Prisons Acts 16:13-40**

Over and over again the powers at work in the world present to us the message that God does not care about us. We go through these times and we can't understand how this could be happening to us. We begin to believe God does not really love us. Of course there can be no more insidious lie. Faith is not wishful thinking or believing that what I want to happen will come to be. Faith is continuing to trust in God—especially when it comes to being released from the prisons holding us.

> Faith is continuing to trust in God—especially when it comes to being released from the prisons holding us.

What is happening in your life to keep you from experiencing complete freedom?

Suggested Spiritual Practice

This will depend on what kind of thing is keeping you from experiencing freedom. If you have financial bondage, you may resolve to take a class on financial freedom during Lent. If an addiction holds you back, maybe it is time to find resources for fighting that addiction. Consider finding a local "Celebrate Recovery" group for support. If you are imprisoned by the belief that God does not love you, you may want to meet regularly with a spiritual counselor to pray through the events that have made you feel that way.

- **Bigger** Psalm 8

We try to make life fit into too small of a box. We try to get our minds around it and so we keep shrinking it down to make it fit within the limits of our awareness. If the reality of Easter is going to launch us out into the wide-open vastness of God's great plans we have to learn to expect more than our imaginations are naturally able to handle. Lent may be a time for meditating on the greatness of God. How could you put that into practice in concrete ways?

Suggested Spiritual Practice

Try spending a few minutes every day praising God for the wonders of the universe. Every time you encounter startling beauty or expansive thoughts, praise God.

- **Habits**

Hanging on to our habits of sin is like trying to drive a car with the parking brake still engaged, or like trying to sail with a line still attached to the dock. Consider what must be cast off in order for you to thrive.

LAUNCH

Suggested Spiritual Practice

This may be a case where simple exertion of the will could win the battle, but cause you to lose the war. You could simply identify a bad habit, like sarcasm or too many sodas, and simply resolve to refrain from that habit during Lent. But so much more good comes if you will instead spend the season of Lent confessing your powerlessness against the temptation of a habit, and then

Are you adding something good, or eliminating something bad?

Generally we grow by adding good habits or practices, and by eliminating the things that are bogging us down or leading in the wrong direction. For example, you may grow in peace by removing stressful things, or by embracing calming elements.

Once you identify the area of growth, consider whether you need to add something to your life, or take something out of your life in order to follow the pattern of the life of Jesus.

What will you add?

What will you remove?

prayerfully discovering God's power to chase that habit away. The difference is subtle, but crucial.

• Do You Do Well To Be Angry?   Jonah 4:9

Some temptations can be conquered by avoidance, some through embracing alternative positive habits. But anger is just there all the time.

Jonah is angry because he does not like what God is doing. He wants revenge. He wants God to annihilate his enemy.

I have gone back and looked at the phrase, "Do you do well to be angry?" (Jonah 4:9) in the original Hebrew. It may be a more accurate to read this question as, "Do you enjoy smoldering?" I know I don't. How could you let go of anger during the season of Lent? It may help to spend the season of Lent meditating on the self-destructiveness of anger. Anger feeds on the false illusion that I will feel better if my enemy suffers.

Suggested Spiritual Practice

This may be a simple as praying, "forgive us our debts as we forgive our debtors," once every day, and then making an effort to mean it.

• The Right Protection Colossians 3:5-14

In his letter to the church at Colossae, Paul urges his friends to put to death certain negative practices, to clothe themselves with several characteristics, and to put on love. Take some time to linger on the meaning of each of these positive characteristics. Do these words describe how you live?

Suggested Spiritual Practice

As you put these verses into practice, consider all aspects of verse 12. Carefully read through the verse word by word. Which of these concepts is most challenging? You might spend Lent putting on these things. Again, spiritual practices involve more than just trying harder. What small steps could you consistently take to put one of these into practice?

- **Impulsiveness** Proverbs 19:2

When is it time to be deliberate and move slowly, and when is it time to act rapidly and boldly? Obviously the answer depends on the situation.

Impulsive people are often rewarded and praised in life because their drive and initiative makes them strong leaders. But sometimes drive and initiative are the result of an inwardly impulsive personality, and that can be trouble.

Only you know what is inside. Lent might be a time to recognize and resist impulsiveness on a daily basis.

Suggested Spiritual Practice

Identifying impulsiveness is a challenge because the impulsive desires themselves tend to block sound reasoning. When you want to go out for ice cream you don't want to be in contact with that part of the brain that evaluates the wisdom of that idea. Rather than trying to fight those thoughts in the heat of the moment it may be better to take on the practice of contentment. Spending a few moments per day reading psalms of praise is one suggestion for how to practice contentment. I would recommend book IV of the Psalms, which is Psalms 90 through 106. You could read one per day. When you get to 106, go back and start back at 90 again. You will make it through about two and a half times during the course of Lent. Spend time thinking about how much God has provided for you. The contentment that results may counteract impulsiveness.

- **Poor Listening** II Corinthians 13:11

As you read through this verse, take a moment to think of all that is packed into each one of the words. It may help to underline the words that speak most powerfully to you, or to list them on a 3x5 card and keep that card in your pocket, reviewing it from time to time during the day.

Good listening is a required first step in putting this verse into practice. Conversely, poor listening will make it impossible to even begin.

Good listening is something to be used in the right way and in the right situation. Don't listen to manipulative or abusive voices. Don't listen to things that tempt you or bring you down. But do listen to others when it may bring reconciliation. Listen for how to make peace. Listen for God's leading in conversations.

Suggested Spiritual Practice

Listen to one person, from your heart, one time every day. You may want to incorporate reminders of this in your prayer time so that you will be ready to listen when the moment arrives.

- **Avoidance** Luke 12:35-40

Avoidance can be a really good way to avert a whole lot of trouble. But some people

Don't get bogged down

There are a lot of suggestions here, but only because there are so many different kinds of people facing different kinds of challenges. Only read these suggestions until you begin to have a sense of how God is challenging you in this season. You might want to use this space to write some notes to yourself about the ideas that are coming to you, and then continue reading the examples.

habitually avoid the things they really should be facing.

Suggested Spiritual Practice

Avoidance may be a result of being too passive. Consider what anxieties might be making you too passive. Consider what one thing you might intentionally confront in order to grow out of the habit of avoidance.

- **Restlessness** Isaiah 28:20

I can't think of a more vivid description of restlessness than Isaiah 28:20. Just as a person cannot violate the laws of nutrition without getting sick, so it is with the moral laws: violation leads to a sickening of the soul, and one symptom of that sickening is restlessness.

Please notice that I did not say, *Restlessness means you have violated some moral law.* I'm sure there are multitudes of reasons for restlessness. And restlessness very well might be the cure for stagnation. It might be the thing that helps you to launch.

So what is it? Are you restless because you know you are engaged in morally questionable things? Are you divided between a balance of the most important pursuits? Are you scattered because you are running around without any sense of why you are doing what you do? Lent might be a time of intentionally resisting restlessness.

Suggested Spiritual Practice

When does restlessness strike you most consistently? Sitting in a meeting at work? Waiting for the mail? Identify the things that make restlessness spike. Pick one to resist intentionally and cultivate calm in that moment. For example, if you find yourself restless in the last hour of your work day, take the season of Lent as a challenge to embrace that hour every day.

Put It Into Practice

- **Do You Want To Be Well?**

    In John 5:6 Jesus asks a man, "Do you want to get well?"

    Why wouldn't a person want to be well? There are as many answers to that question as there are people. Lent could be a time of discovering true healing.

Suggested Spiritual Practice

These may be questions that should not be explored alone. See if you can find a wise, trained, and experienced person to explore these questions together with you. Then, together you may find an action you can take throughout Lent to begin the healing.

- **Afraid To Ask** Matthew 7:7-11

    Heartbreaks aren't usually healed until they are exposed. Lost dreams aren't found unless reported missing. Yearnings to start over may never come to anything until they are spoken out loud in prayer. Yet some people are afraid to give voice to those requests. Are you afraid to ask God for the deepest desires in your heart?

Suggested Spiritual Practice

Take a few moments to jot down the disappointments you have with God. What do your disappointments have in common? Is there a theme of unanswered requests? Have you persevered in "having it out" with God? How might the next several weeks be a time of learning to be honest in prayer?

- **Finding Peace** Psalm 131

    This Psalm is all about knowing when to be content inside limits. Gratitude is like a handle that lifts you out of all of your striving and frenetic longing. Gratitude takes you to a different place. When this psalm says, "I have stilled and quieted my soul;" it means "I have grown so calm that my breathing is deep and relaxed."

LAUNCH

Following Jesus isn't just a matter of the mind or the will, it is meant to have an effect on the body.

We say we want peace, but yet we find ourselves fidgety whenever we get the opportunity to be still and rest. Is this season of Lent a time for you to rest?

Suggested Spiritual Practice

Consider how deep peace is rooted in your relationship with God. You may want to spend Lent reflecting on the nature of God as a way of growing more content in God's peace. God created us, and so he has every right to give us whatever life he wants to give us. And when we rebel against that we say, "God, you had no right to make me the way I am." Or, "Why couldn't I have been taller, or better looking, or smarter, or richer?"

And God says, "You never will find peace until you accept that I made you just the way I wanted you to be."

God is the creator of everything, and as creator, he has every right to fashion us and our lives however he might choose.

Then when I think of Jesus, I think of what a mess I made of my life without him. And when I was completely stuck, with no hope in this world, Jesus reached down and just lifted me out of the mess I made. Consider what your life is–that everything you have is beyond what you could have made for yourself. Gratitude takes you to a different place.

And then there is the third person of the trinity, the Holy Spirit. The Holy Spirit is God's constant presence, always ready to bring calm in any storm, always ready to answer if we will just cry out.

Spend Lent in reflection on these things in order to grow in peace.

• **Pruning** John 15:1-17

Put It Into Practice

It is surprising to walk through a pruned vineyard. Sometime in the middle of winter the pruners work their way through vines, trimming massive amounts of branch. In my ignorance I cannot help but feel the excessiveness of the pruning when I see the result. "That can't be good for the plant. Someone made a mistake. Boy is he going to get fired for doing that to these precious vines."

But come back as the summer progresses and you will discover this pruning was exactly what the vine needed to thrive. A good pruning pushes all of the growth into the fruit. How might God be using events in your life to prune away the bad?

Suggested Spiritual Practice

Here is where the spiritual practices of abstaining from something can be helpful. Fasting is one variety of the refraining practices. This could involve choosing to forego one meal per week, or it could mean giving up a favorite food for the season of Lent. But there are also many more forms of abstaining that could be helpful for you. Consider giving up television, video games, social media, caffeine, alcohol, or anything that feels like an important crutch for your life. If you find yourself getting mad at me for mentioning one of those, that might be a clue as to which one needs to go. Remember to be careful about noticing when pride enters, and keep the main purpose in mind. You are giving something up in order to make space for God to grow something better in its place.

LAUNCH

Personal Commitment Notes
Use this space to jot down notes to yourself.

What is the one area of your spiritual life that you feel God is calling you to address in order to launch into a new way of serving him?

What daily, measurable practice are you choosing to put into place in order to grow in this area?

How do you imagine your life will be different after Easter as God blesses you with growth in this area?

What are some daily reminders that you can put into place so that you will remember to engage consistently in this practice?

Who are some of the people in your life who could help encourage you to keep going if this grows difficult?

What are some of the things you could ask those people to do in order to encourage you?

4
Ash Wednesday

Burning Palms, Burning Hearts

The Spirit of the Sovereign Lord is on me,
    because the Lord has anointed me
    to proclaim good news to the poor.
He has sent me to bind up the brokenhearted,
    to proclaim freedom for the captives
    and release from darkness for the prisoners,
to proclaim the year of the Lord's favor
    and the day of vengeance of our God,
to comfort all who mourn,
    and provide for those who grieve in Zion—
to bestow on them a crown of beauty
    instead of ashes,
the oil of joy
    instead of mourning,
and a garment of praise
    instead of a spirit of despair.
They will be called oaks of righteousness,
    a planting of the Lord
    for the display of his splendor.

Isaiah 61:1-3

Ash Wednesday

It is my hope that your journey through Lent will have the effect of launching you out into life at its fullest in a lifelong journey of truly following Jesus. Lent begins with Ash Wednesday. Traditionally the ashes for Ash Wednesday are made by burning the palms from last year's celebration of Palm Sunday. The leftover palms gradually shrivel and dry over the course of a year, until what was a vibrant symbol of life becomes a dead and hardened image of the way things go in this world. Just before Ash Wednesday those dead palms are burned to make ashes as a visible sign of our sin and our mortality. On Palm Sunday Jesus entered Jerusalem to shouts of triumph. Many churches celebrated that triumph by waving palms in a great processional on Palm Sunday last year. We remembered also how Jesus looked out over Jerusalem and wept for it, because the people had not recognized how God had been among them.

Not only do dried palms make a really good ash when burned, but also the symbolism involved points toward the meaning of Ash Wednesday. All of the effort to make ourselves into virtuous people, waving our palm branches and blending with the crowd of Jesus fans, eventually leads to a shriveled up leaf best used for creating a symbol of death. Lent is an annual spiritual practice of letting our past efforts die in order

The Plan

Read this section to prepare for Ash Wednesday.

to take up the new quest constantly offered to us by our ever-creative God.

We begin Lent with a reflection on our own mortality at Ash Wednesday because understanding the limits of our lives can wake us up to the need to jettison things of lesser importance. We are reminded to stop wallowing in the misery of our shortcomings. The world is bigger than our own private perspectives. This purging is intended to leave us in a position to clearly see and embrace God's transforming power.

> I consider that our present sufferings are not worth comparing with the glory that will be revealed in us.
>
> Romans 8:18

The Apostle Paul wrote, "I consider that our present sufferings are not worth comparing with the glory that will be revealed in us." (Romans 8:18)

Some suffering arises out of random acts and uncontrollable misfortune. Some suffering stems from unmitigated evil perpetrated by bad people. Some suffering is the unintended consequence of an otherwise neutral action. And some suffering comes from love. To love someone hurts. Love means exposing yourself to pain.

In spite of the pain of love, the alternative is numbness, which is a kind of death. Those who choose not to experience the pain of love are living to some degree in a denial of God. Even though the pain of love seems like something that will kill us, it is in loving that we find life. To be human is to love. To be human is to lose. Those who do not love may escape the pain of love, but they deny the image of God in themselves and suffer in the shriveled up world of numbness.

Ash Wednesday

So this may sound really odd, but that is why Ash Wednesday and Valentine's Day go perfectly together. Because of the quirks of the calendar, Ash Wednesday and St. Valentine's Day will fall on the same day in 2018, 2024, and 2029. This has not happened even once since at least 1992, and won't happen again after 2029 for a very long time. This represents a unique kind of conflict because Valentine's Day is often celebrated with decadent consumption dedicated to the pursuit of romantic love, while Ash Wednesday points to austere reflection on the transitory nature of the things of this world. Yet can it be that Ash Wednesday and St. Valentine's Day shed pools of light on one another? Love is painful. Pain is better than numbness. Love is worth the suffering. The love of Jesus turns the ashes of our failures into the beauty of redemption.

Questions for Reflection

Ash Wednesday services often include time for repentance, and ashes in the sign of a cross as a reminder of our mortality and sinfulness. Are you attracted to a service with those elements or are you repulsed by those things?

What is it about those elements that either attracts you or repulses you?

5

First Week of Lent

The Wedge

. . . let us draw near to God with a sincere heart and with the full assurance that faith brings, having our hearts sprinkled to cleanse us from a guilty conscience and having our bodies washed with pure water.

Hebrews 10:22

The Wedge

I love outdoor survival and wilderness shows. Once I watched a man make cross-country skis for himself out of a tree using nothing but hand tools. First he selected the tree with the straightest trunk and cut it down. Then he drove a steel wedge at a certain angle upward through the grain from the bottom of the tree. As he pounded the wedge into the round base of the trunk we watched as the wood split along the grain a little at a time. But then a sort of cracking sound signaled that a board was splitting out. He repeated the process and soon he had two boards split from the trunk of the tree.

It was amazing to see how a wedge driven in at one end of the trunk could cause a crack all of the way along the grain, so that each board was easily split out of the log.

Life does that to people. A wedge is driven between God and us. It may start with a shallow penetration of a seemingly harmless thought. It may begin with a little event that at first only penetrates an inch or two. But some

> ### The Plan
>
> This chapter is for the first week of Lent—that is, sometime during the week following the first Sunday in Lent. This week you will be considering what things come as a barrier in between you and God. Read this section and consider how God might be using Lent as a way of breaking down those barriers.

45

thoughts or events inevitably cause a crack along the entire grain.

The wedge is different for different people. For some it is guilt and disappointment. These people might sense that God is not pleased with how they are living their lives so they avoid God, and they get a little bit angry when God enters a conversation. Others are disappointed by the way God has not taken care of them. Still others want freedom and they feel that if God were to be consulted life would get smaller, more confined, and they don't want that. Doubt can be a wedge too, though it does not have to be. Doubt used well is more often a way of growth and need not become a wedge. Yet often it does.

In truth, none of these things necessarily become wedges. Remember that a wedge is something that starts in a shallow way but becomes the sort of thing that makes a person unable to relate to God in an honest, straightforward way. Truth be told, for some pastors and religious leaders the whole life of serving God by leading people can itself ironically become a wedge that leads to separation from God.

> ... a wedge is something that starts in a shallow way but becomes the sort of thing that makes a person unable to relate to God in an honest, straightforward way.

It sounds strange, but really anything can be a wedge. It is the great variety of wedges that leads me to believe something larger and darker is at work. This is more than the power of a guilty habit or the healthy wondering of a skeptical mind. Something is at work in us and in the world to take events and turn them into wedges–cascading separators that cause a split along our whole way of relating to God.

The Wedge

Three stories in the Bible show what this wide variety of wedges all have in common. These are all familiar stories, so let me just summarize and show you what I mean. The first story happened in the Garden of Eden when the serpent confronted Adam and Eve. People often think of this as a temptation story, but it is really a wedge story. Adam and Eve were living so naturally in the presence of God that they didn't even think it unusual to take a walk together with him. The serpent did not really tempt them—or at least, that is not the main thing that happened in the story. The serpent questioned whether or not God really had their best interest at heart. When that question was introduced it did not appear to be significant at first. Like a steel wedge a few inches into the heartwood of a tree, the question itself did not change things very much. As events unfolded, as the wedge created a crack along the grain of the relationship, eventually all was changed and there they stood, two unconnected boards. Only then was it clear that the wedge had done its work.

Likewise in the story of Job, the question, *Would Job be faithful to God if he went through tremendous suffering?* became a wedge along the whole of the relationship between God and Job. Only when God tore apart the curtain separating heaven and earth and revealed himself to Job did the wedge begin to heal.

Jesus also was subjected to this same steel. Having spent forty days in the desert alone and fasting, Jesus was subjected to three wedge questions. Are you really the Son of God? Will God really care for you? Isn't there an easier way to come into your kingdom?

Since even Jesus took a pounding all of us who carry around the reality of a wedge all of the time should take heart. Even Jesus felt the crack of that steel. And yet he managed to resist the split and endure the pounding without letting the crack run its course. This is one of the ways Jesus is very different from every other person who has ever lived.

LAUNCH

Wedges are real and inevitable, yet relief must be possible too. If Easter this year is going to be your chance to launch out into the ocean of God's love, it may be necessary to identify the wedge (or wedges) that keep you from living in close relationship with God. You are not able to remove the wedge by yourself. But God is actively working to remove those barriers, and Lent is a time for beginning to let him do it.

The Wedge

Reflection Questions

Read Ephesians 2:11-18

What are some of the dividing walls that keep people separated from one another and from God?

Name one "dividing wall" in the world that you would most like to see come down.

How does the gospel break down religious and social dividing walls?

What is your role in helping the people in your community show unity in Christ?

What walls do you need Christ to knock down in order for you be reconciled with others?

The entire second chapter of Ephesians is filled with some of the most encouraging words ever written. Have you ever memorized any of these verses?

Verses 12 and 13 contain a shorter version of the emphasis of the whole chapter. How would you summarize this message in your own words?

Verse 12 is very bleak. Have you ever felt yourself to be separated like this?

LAUNCH

Launching in Lent

What are some of the wedges that people sometimes experience in their relationship with God?

How do your daily habits help you grow closer to God?

Is it possible to get rid of bad habits or grow into a better person but also become separated from God?

Consider the one spiritual practice you have chosen for Lent. How does that one practice help you grow closer to God? Are you ever tempted to engage in that spiritual practice in a way that actually drives you farther away from God? How might you change your approach to make this into a bridge rather than a wedge?

6

Second Week of Lent

Leaving Your City Behind

By faith Abraham, when called to go to a place he would later receive as his inheritance, obeyed and went, even though he did not know where he was going. By faith he made his home in the promised land like a stranger in a foreign country; he lived in tents, as did Isaac and Jacob, who were heirs with him of the same promise. For he was looking forward to the city with foundations, whose architect and builder is God.

Hebrews 11:8-10

We tend to remember the tower of Babel described in Genesis 11:4, but we tend not to remember that the people built a *city* and a tower, and the purpose was to create an identity for themselves. Both the city and the tower represent the will of the people to govern their own lives in rebellion against the idea of being lovingly ruled by the will of God.

As the Bible moves on from the tower of Babel episode, God calls Abram out of his city into a new land that God would show him (Genesis 12:1). The book of Hebrews stresses the importance of Abraham's motivations.

When Jesus gathered people, he often brought them together outside of the cities they came from. The constant theme of both his actions and his teaching was the formation of a new community, what he calls "the Kingdom of Heaven." We hear that and forget that in those days kings were primarily kings over cities, not nations. So when Jesus would say, "The kingdom of heaven is like . . ." all of the people listening would be imagining a spiritual city.

In many different ways, the city represents our

> ## The Plan
>
> This week you will consider the community immediately around you. Read this section and consider how the culture around you may be keeping you from growing.

identity and our allegiance. Jesus calls us out of our self-created identities, and invites us to take up his identity, to be part of his city. We can't really do that until we have left behind the identity formed by the community around us. Because if we embrace the identity of our surrounding communities we will act in certain ways, but if we live with our allegiance to another city–the spiritual city where Jesus reigns–we will live in different ways. Once extracted from our cities we are pointed toward God's eternal city. Being identified with Christ we are then compelled to re-engage our communities with the transforming love of Christ.

God sees us in our future and is always calling to us. He invites us to leave the old behind, and to reach out for the new identity he continually offers. If we see ourselves as God sees us, in our future, calling us toward how he already knows we will be, our lives will grow to be more and more like how he sees us. The God who has no trouble overcoming impossibilities is making all things new. He longs to start today, in you and in me, proclaiming an end to this chapter and a new chapter beginning. God is saying to you today that it is time to bring the water of life to a thirsty land. It is time to feed the hungry from the tree of life. It is time to be the healing for the nations.

But none of that can happen unless we leave our cities behind. God is asking us to leave behind our allegiance to our places of origin. This is not because God is indifferent to the hurting and struggling world around us. In fact, the opposite is true. God cares for our communities more than we do. But we can't bring lasting help to our struggling communities until God has detached us from the tangles of their decay.

Questions for Reflection

Read Hebrews 11:8-10

What were some of the things Abraham enjoyed that he had to leave behind? (See Genesis 12:1 for some ideas.)

What are some of the benefits of living in the same place all of your life?

Read Luke 9:51-62

What are some of the things that people are required to leave behind in order to follow Jesus?

What does each of these things represent?

Which of these do you feel most? That is, which would be the hardest for you to leave behind?

Launching in Lent

As you look at the week ahead, do you see any ways that you will be challenged to let go of something in order to follow Jesus? Will you need to separate yourself from the crowd around you?

What resources do you have to stay faithful under that kind of pressure?

7

Third Week of Lent

Comparison

A heart at peace gives life to the body, but envy rots the bones.

Proverbs 14:30

Comparison

One story in the Bible highlights the problem of comparison. Genesis 25:24-26 describes the births of twin boys briefly. The two sons are locked into a competition from the beginning. Esau wins the first race in life by positioning. That is, he is born first so all of the rights and privileges of the oldest son immediately fall to him. Jacob is born minutes later. As though he knows that this was a race (of course a baby never could know that, right?) Jacob is born clutching the heel of his older brother like a defensive back committing pass interference. Jacob and Esau are very different from birth. We can imagine their father, Isaac, putting a bow and arrow into Esau's hands and sending him out on his adventures, while their mother, Rebekah, pulls Jacob into her tent to protect and to nurture him, to show him he is special and to teach him about the things that matter most to her.

Esau and Jacob are divided from each other along the fault lines of their parents' standoff. A picture of two tents, a "his" and a

The Plan

Comparison can be deadly. This week consider your own challenges of comparison. How might God be leading you to leave comparison behind in this season of preparation for Easter.

"hers," describes the way Isaac and Rebekah relate to one another, so also is it fitting that they have twin boys, one child per parent. Children feel the problems and tensions between their parents.

This picture of divided parents and divided siblings is just an easy illustration of the way conflicts often get started in many families. It's just not always so obvious. When the marriage is not going so well and both husband and wife are secretly frightened to face the problems between them they often withdraw from paying attention to the marriage and focus on the children. "If our marriage isn't what I was hoping for, maybe I can compensate by making a good family," they say inside. They turn all of their energy into controllable factors of family success. Parents typically throw themselves into their work to advance the financial well-being of the family, or they focus on raising the children with solid values as they redouble their efforts to guide the children toward a successful future. But what is ignored in the marriage is often driven more deeply into the children as Isaac and Rebekah have done. They can't help but take out the anxieties of their incompatibility on the boys. Soon Esau comes to be a living metaphor of Isaac's wish to escape—he is only happy when he is out in the field away from the home. Jacob comes to represent Rebekah's objection to everything wrong with Isaac but in a twisted way. While Isaac is passive, Jacob becomes aggressively grabby, treating everything that can be acquired as his personal property. Eventually this conflict leads Jacob, under his mother's influence, to commit an unforgivable treachery by stealing the blessing of the Father reserved for the first-born. Rebekah pulls the strings in the situation to obtain favor for her favorite son. Ultimately she achieves for Jacob what she cannot have herself: the freedom to go back home to the tent of her brother and put this whole bad marriage behind her.

The problems between the parents have a corrosive effect on the developing personalities of the two boys. Notice how each of the brothers in the situation is made to feel only halfway accepted. The trouble with comparisons comes in the human tendency to obsessively long for whatever is missing. After all Esau probably is not saying to himself, "Dad loves me." He is probably saying to himself, "What is wrong with me that my mother loves Jacob better?"

So also Jacob wonders why he can never please his father, why his father treats him as though he were invisible. All of this would be confusing to an adult, so how much more are children puzzled by these events? Arbitrary unwritten rules govern the family causing some to be more favored than others. But no one ever explains the rules. Jacob just knows his dad likes his brother better, and his mom won't let him out of the tent, but Esau gets to go out wherever he wants to go. They are exactly the same age except for a few minutes, but because of the cultural rules of inheritance Esau will become the patriarch of the family when Isaac dies and Jacob will forever be the one who bows and serves. That initial race to be born first turned out to really matter.

No wonder the two boys grow apart from one another but are careening on an inevitable collision course. The boys are locked into competition and they will certainly suffer because of the constant tendency for comparison. Competition and comparison are different things but they tend to be intertwined with one another. Competition is good and usually works to make everyone better. Competition pushes us to be our best. And besides, competition is fun. A softball game with no scorekeeping eventually dissolves into a mess. The drive to compete against a worthy opponent brings challenge and excitement to many different things in life. But in many ways we suffer from destructive comparisons as a result of competition. State champion swimmers only regard themselves as the ones who failed to reach the Olympics. Perfectly beautiful young women only see themselves as larger than the models on the cover of the magazines. While competition is good, destructive comparisons can become debilitating and can ruin lives.

Think for a moment of a time when you were disappointed with yourself. Were you disappointed that you had not made more of a success of yourself in your career? Were you frustrated about your weight or fitness? Did you berate yourself for not being smart enough to solve a particular problem? It is very likely that your picture of yourself as a failure has another person in it who succeeded. Career frustrations arise when someone younger is promoted above us, or when we go to a class reunion and hear what our classmates have done with their lives. We hate our bodies when we see someone who has a really nice one. We think we are dumb when someone else seems smarter.

Do you see how it works? We are always comparing ourselves to one another, and we all manage to feel inferior. Only rarely does anyone ever feel superior by comparison. In fact, most of the people who look like winners in the world are constantly chasing an inward sense of inferiority. None of the "wins" ever extinguishes the inner ache of a deep sense of inferiority. A momentary victory may come, a time when comparison boosts the ego. But soon winners become addicted to winning. They can't stand to lose, ever. A mask of security is fashioned to cover a dark fear that to lose is to fall into despair.

> . . . Do not think of yourself more highly than you ought, but rather think of yourself with sober judgment, in accordance with the faith God has distributed to each of you.
>
> Romans 12:3

Comparison

Jacob and Esau were each raised on the praise of a parent. But that praise only made them each feel inferior. Even complimentary comparisons pave the way for feelings of inferiority. Imagine Isaac and Esau out in the field for Esau's first hunting trip. They carefully stalk their prey until they are close enough for a shot. Esau slips an arrow from his quiver, carefully draws back the string of his bow and lets the arrow fly. For an instant it appears the young hunter will see success, but the arrow sticks into the ground just wide of the target. The startled animal scurries away, out of range. Isaac is disappointed. But he doesn't want to discourage his son so he says, "That was a very good shot for a boy of your age, Esau."

Esau looks dejected but doesn't say anything. Isaac tries harder. "Don't worry son, you will soon be bringing in lots of meat for the family. It just takes time. A lot of boys your age would just give up right now, but you are not like them. I know you will get out here and keep practicing with that bow, and sooner or later you will be walking home with a fat gazelle on your shoulders."

Isaac wants to encourage his son in a time of disappointment. He wants to find a way to console Esau in a moment that is a failure in reality. So how can he rescue the boy from feeling like he is a failure after one isolated experience of failure? The easiest way is by comparison. And most of us take that easy way most of the time.

And it probably works. Very likely the father and son will enjoy a special bond prompted by those encouraging words. And don't get me wrong: this is better than criticizing. Esau will feel better, and he will be more likely to try again until he finds success. But on the deepest level he is on his way to being addicted to the habit of measuring his worth in comparison with the people around him rather than by knowing he is loved because God made him well. If Esau truly learns this lesson he will begin to console himself in all of his troubles by looking for someone around him who is worse. If he makes a mistake he will look for someone who has made a bigger mistake. If his arrow finds its mark in a really large prize specimen of game his joy will be contained until he goes home and asks if this is the biggest anyone has ever killed. And while he recognizes that his father loves him best, he can't help but notice that his mother loves his brother best. The relative lack of love from his mother probably tears Esau down more than the love of his father builds him up.

But this is Jacob's story, not Esau's so let's see how the problem of comparison affects the younger brother in the story. Jacob clearly has the love of his mother but knows he will always be second son to his father. As a result he develops the habit of constantly scheming to displace his brother. And Rebekah, the twins' mother, continually fuels this fire. She seems to be working out all of the unhappiness of her own life by advancing the fortunes of her favorite son.

> ## Bible Passages related to comparison
>
> Philippians 2:3
> Romans 12:10
> Matthew 20:1-16

We all carry around inside of our heads an idea of what we were supposed to become. Jacob is a little different from most people in that he has an actual twin brother living in the favor of their father while he can only console himself with the comfort of his mother.

It is important to confront the problem of comparison because in some foundational way, no one is ready to receive the news of Easter until the habit of comparison has been jettisoned

Comparison

completely. There is an old saying, The ground is level at the foot of the cross. To be ready to go to the foot of the cross involves accepting the meaninglessness of all comparisons.

The resurrection of Jesus is a gift. Nothing ruins a gift more swiftly than comparison. If you are going to launch in to the power of the resurrection you must let go of comparison.

Questions for Reflection

Read James 3:13-18

What negative behaviors does James list? What positive characteristics?

Do you know people who show their wisdom through humility?

What is it like to be around them?

How does comparison lead to envy?

What are some of the dangers of comparison?

Do you ever feel cheated and neglected by God if someone nearby enjoys some advantage over you–like someone who has a nicer house, a more prestigious job, or a beautiful singing voice?

Launching in Lent

Some compare themselves to others in envy. Others often feel good about themselves if they compare favorably to those around them.

LAUNCH

Either way, this is a form of what James calls being "double-minded." (James 1:8 and 4:8)

How do you see comparison as part of being "double-minded"?

In many ways the antidote for comparison comes in true worship of God. How does worship of God relieve you of the burden of comparison?

If comparison has gotten out of hand, how can you make a determined effort in the coming week to thank God that no one else is like you?

Do you need to repent of a tendency to compare your life to others?

What kind of steps can you take to let wisdom turn into humility in the coming week?

8

Fourth Week of Lent

Emptiness

"My people have committed two sins:
They have forsaken me,
    the spring of living water,
and have dug their own cisterns,
    broken cisterns that cannot hold water."
        Jeremiah 2:13

Emptiness

I spent one summer during my college years painting houses to earn enough money to stay in school. I did this in my hometown of Richland, Washington. Now Richland is in the desert part of the state of Washington, and summer temperatures often reach 110 degrees or more. We were painting outside and we couldn't afford to call off the day's labor during the weeks when temperatures soared above 100. On those days there was something especially good about turning on the garden hose and pointing it straight up in the air and taking a drink from the flowing water.

Flowing water is always best, but in arid regions it is sometimes necessary to build cisterns to store water from the rainy season to last through droughts. In Israel there are ancient cisterns built into the sides of mountains. People constructed canals to channel the rainwater into giant underground storage pools so that water would always be available regardless of the precipitation of the season.

It only takes a small crack to make a cistern worthless. Water has that relentless tendency to drain away steadily through any opening.

The Plan

This week you will be considering if some of your habits are aimed at filling a void that can never really be filled.

LAUNCH

A 16,000 gallon cistern only needs to lose 2 gallons per hour to go to zero before the year is out.

Most people wrestle with a hole in their cistern. Of course when I say this I mean their cistern is their soul and the hole is that condition we all know when nothing can really ever fill the draining emptiness, the endless thirst of a soul with a crack. We see the results in overeating, in pornography addictions, in alcohol abuse. People get dragged into sins of indulgence not because they have a hunger that isn't filled, but because they have a hunger that can't be filled. The very things used to fill the hunger actually make the hole in the cistern bigger.

In the novel, The Brothers Karamazov, Fyodor Dostoevsky inserts a parable about an onion as the characters talk about greed. Some of you will have a hard time considering the meaning of this parable because it will seem to violate your theology of salvation. Without denying the importance of good theology I would ask you to put that analysis on pause for long enough to consider the parable from a different angle.

The parable goes like this.

Once there was a woman who was as selfish and bitter as could be, and she died. She left not one good deed behind her throughout her whole life. Demons took her and threw her into the lake of fire. The woman had a guardian angel who had watched over her all of her life and he asked himself, *What one good deed from this woman's life can I remember so that I may tell God?*

As he stood pondering he remembered and spoke to God about it. He said, "Once she dug an onion from her garden and gave it to a beggar woman."

God answered, "Take the same onion she gave away and hold it out to her over the lake. Let her get hold of the onion and pull. If you are able to pull her out of the lake with the onion then she may enter paradise. But if the onion breaks she will have to remain in the lake of fire."

The angel hurried to the woman and held out her onion to her. "Here," he said, "grab onto the onion and I will pull you."

He began to carefully pull and had nearly pulled her out. When the other sinners in the lake saw her being pulled they all began holding onto the woman, hoping they could be pulled out too. But the wickedness of the woman took over and she started kicking all of the other sinners. "Let go," she shouted, "this is my onion, not yours."

The instant she said that the onion broke and the woman fell back into the lake of fire and is still burning there. Her angel wept and slowly walked away.

The onion broke because of the selfishness of the woman, not from the weight of the other sinners. And while I don't believe our rescue from the eternal misery of our sin depends on our deeds to pull us out of the lake of fire, this parable is told as an insight into spiritual growth in life. Acts of selfishness can sink us.

The story in Mark 12:41-44 raises the importance of generosity, even in small things. Jesus watches a poor widow give a small gift of two copper coins and then he tells the disciples that she has given more than anyone else. The contribution of the widow was so small as to make no material difference in the outcome of the collection efforts. Those two tiny copper coins are not going to raise the total much. Jesus is pointing to the importance of generosity in the life of the giver. In contrast, holding on tightly to what is mine might just sever the cord that is dragging me out of my misery.

This kind of selfishness points to an inner hunger that can never be filled. Like the cistern with a crack, the selfish person who has a hard time giving to others is incessantly grasping for anything in sight in order to fill an ever-waning inner sense of contentment.

LAUNCH

Many people who are vulnerable to temptations of all kinds try to resist temptation by force of will. They simply cut themselves off from whatever indulgence tempts them. That does not work and sometimes makes things worse. That may enlarge the crack in the cistern—the deep inner part of the soul that constantly allows all good things to drain away. The solution is obvious, even though it may be difficult. First repair the crack, and then resistance to all kinds of temptation will follow naturally. Here is where a wise and trusted friend or spiritual counselor could be of great help. Try to find someone who is confidential and who can listen and help you find the reason all good things disappear from your soul. With support, find ways of focusing attention on God's abundance rather than on what you feel you lack.

As I write this I am praying for you, that you will find abundance that lasts.

Emptiness

Questions for Reflection

Read I Timothy 6:3-10

Consider the person described in I Timothy 6:3-5. What is a good word to describe the emotional state of this person?

Paul contrasts the person of verses 3-5 with a different type of person in verses 6-10. What is the contrasting emotional state of this second person?

Can you name a time when your great desire for something got you into trouble?

What are some things you can do in order to increase your contentment?

Launching in Lent

Who is someone that you admire for their generous spirit? Have you ever asked that person what motivates her or him to give so freely? What is one thing you could do to follow that person's example?

9

Fifth Week of Lent

Knowing Hope

. . . as the anchor is cast through the waters into a dark and unseen place, and while it lies hid there, keeps the vessel beaten by the waves from being overwhelmed; so must our hope be fixed on the invisible God.

John Calvin, Epistle to the Hebrews, Chapter VI 19.

The beginning of my adult life of faith came when I was 16 years old. I was confronted with the question, "If you believe in Jesus Christ, then why don't you live as though you do?"

In essence, the whole idea of getting ready for Easter means taking an honest look at that gap between what I say I believe and what I actually do.

If this question had come from someone else then I probably would have dug my heels in, argued, and spun myself into a web of talk and discussion. But the question came from somewhere inside of me, and I believe it was posed to me by God. I could sense and anticipate the liberation and the peace that would come if my actions matched the deepest convictions of my heart.

So the question

The Plan

There may be nothing more consoling than the image of the anchor as used in Hebrews 6:19. God's promise is compared to an anchor as the source of stability in stormy weather.

Read this section and consider how God might be teaching you to rely on real hope in this season of preparation for Easter.

of Easter is not primarily a question of what we believe. It is not "Could Jesus have been raised from the dead?" But rather, "What will I do about the faith that is he is moving inside of me since he is alive?"

The virtue required to put belief into practice is daunting.

Paul wrote to the Church in Ephesus, "I pray also that the eyes of your heart may be enlightened in order that you may know the hope to which he has called you, the riches of his glorious inheritance in the saints, and his incomparably great power for us who believe. That power is like the working of his mighty strength, which he exerted in Christ when he raised him from the dead and seated him at his right hand in the heavenly realms, far above all rule and authority, power and dominion, and every title that can be given, not only in the present age but also in the one to come." -Ephesians 1:18-21

What Paul prayed for the Ephesian Church I pray for us as well. May our hope be rooted in the power of God.

Now with a good understanding of hope established consider for a moment the opposite: Hopelessness.

One summer several years ago I was on vacation in Anaheim, California. My family and I were waiting for a table at a restaurant and I was wearing my souvenir Seattle Mariners baseball jersey. As we stood there the host asked me if I was a fan of the Mariners and what I thought of my team that year. I talked for a few minutes about my favorite players and then I asked him if he was a fan of the Anaheim Angels.

His face turned into a weather phenomenon. A rain cloud covered his whole face and a lightning bolt flashed from his mouth. "I don't cheer for losers," he said.

At that moment the Angels were a long and continuing disappointment. In all of the years of their history they had never gone to a world series, and as we spoke they were in third place in the division behind my Mariners and the red-hot Oakland A's.

The outburst of that host was a common reaction to years of miserable experiences. He was tired of having good expectations for losers.

What he did not know, of course, was that the Angels were about to stage one of the most amazing come from behind seasons of all time. Three months later they surprised everyone by winning their first world series.

This chance conversation with an Angel's non-fan is an example of hopelessness.

Hopelessness means not believing there are good things for you in the future. I contrast this with despair, which I see as believing there are bad things headed for you in the future. In a moment we will turn to despair. The two seem fundamentally different to me, though the result is very similar. Both hopelessness and despair take over the outcome by stealing our motivation to care and to take action.

It is very important for hope to be centered in the truth of what God is doing in you. In a very real way hope reaches from the future backwards to where you are in the present. Hope changes you and makes you ready and able to walk into the goodness God has in store for you. Hopelessness is deadly. Have nothing to do with it. It will freeze you in the icy immobility that will make itself true by what it does to you.

As I wrote above, I see a difference between hopelessness and despair. This distinction may only exist in my small mind, but think about this for a moment and see if you think it is true. I see hopelessness as the belief that nothing good lies in the future. And I see despair as fear that bad things in the future are inescapable.

Even if you are prone to neither of these tendencies, think about your own motivations for a moment. Are you more motivated by the hope of something good, or by the desire to escape something bad? Does fear of punishment get you to live in certain ways, or does hope of reward move you? Or maybe a combination of both?

Some people aren't going anywhere, primarily because of fear. Fear can be paralyzing. If I am afraid I can become completely immobile so that I can't do anything about solving the problem that has me so afraid.

Calvin has written (commentary, Zephaniah 3:7) "And it is what we also know by experience, that when fear prevails in our hearts we are as it were lifeless, so that we cannot raise even a finger to do anything: but when hope animates us, there is a vigour in the whole body, . . ."

From what I have read of Calvin's biography and his letters to friends, I feel he writes about fear from personal experience. If you struggle with fear then I urge you to keep certain passages of scripture nearby at all times. Read Psalm 23, Matthew 6:25-34, Matthew 10:26-31, and 2 Corinthians 7:5-7 and keep them near. Find the passages that most effectively quench your fear and read them as often as is necessary to cast off fear.

Your notes:

Are you immobilized by fear? What is making you afraid?

Questions for Reflection

Read I Peter 1:3-9

According to this passage, what motivates God to give us hope?

What images in this passage emphasize the permanence of our hope?

What are the barriers to seeing the hope God offers us?

According to Ephesians 1:18-21, the main reason for our hope centers around two closely related aspects of God's character: his power and his love. His power means he is able to bless you, and his love means he is willing to bless you. Do you believe in both of those aspects of God's character?

Does doubt of either of those two things ever make you lose hope?

Launching in Lent

Take a moment to think about the spiritual practice you have decided to add to your life throughout Lent. At this point you may be feeling really good because you have consistently stayed with your plan. Or you may have given up your plan.

How does hope enter into your efforts? If your practice has fallen by the wayside, consider your motivations. Is there a way to start back up again now?

10

Holy Week

Make The Most of These Eight Days

Then he called the crowd to him along with his disciples and said: "Whoever wants to be my disciple must deny themselves and take up their cross and follow me."
    Mark 8:34

Make The Most Of These Eight Days

This was an intense week in the life of Jesus, and I'm not just talking about Friday. Consider two questions that spring from the events of the Bible this week. Can you hear the stones? Is it I?

Can You Hear the Stones? Luke 19:29-44

Tensions were high when Jesus entered Jerusalem on the Sunday before Passover. He had arranged his entrance to deliberately send a message, and every year pastors all over the world labor to unfold the nature of that message for their congregations. It is not an easy task. Jesus was entirely clear about what he was saying with his actions. But those who were watching him and who were trying to understand the significance of his actions seem to have missed his message.

Palm Sunday often leaves people with more questions than answers. Yet some questions are distracting. They don't launch us out searching for a truer meaning. Some questions tend to make people stop searching or send us off in unproductive circles. But this one Palm Sunday question pushes me in the right direction every year. Can you hear the stones?

The Plan

This week you may want to attend Maundy Thursday and Good Friday Services.

LAUNCH

This Palm Sunday question arises as I puzzle over one cryptic saying of Jesus. With tensions high, as Jesus rode into Jerusalem on a donkey, the crowd of people on the road began to shout and sing Psalm 118. Some observers, who did not understand what Jesus was about, were worried that Jesus was setting himself up to be crowned king right then and there.

Luke reports that the Pharisees reacted by telling Jesus to get things under control and tone down the chants of the crowd. But Jesus replied that it wouldn't do any good. If his followers were silent the rocks would start shouting.

What could he mean by that? Is it just exaggeration? Maybe it is an old saying. But if so, what does it mean?

Given the power for questions to send us out looking, it may not be best for me to answer. But let me make a few suggestions about where you might go searching for your answers. Jesus may be referring to Psalm 19:1-4, where the Psalmist says that if we could only listen to God's creation we would in some actual way hear what God has made praising him. Or he could be making reference to the book of Habakkuk, which makes the point in a number of different ways that our efforts to twist meanings by shaping natural things into the images of our own invention often make those objects less able to speak truly (Compare Habakkuk 2:11 with 2:18). Because this Palm procession took place in the shadow of the huge stones of the temple, and because the crowd is shouting lines from Psalm 118, I believe the stones Jesus is talking about are the stones of the temple. The temple represents the best efforts of God's people to faithfully worship him. The work of our hands becomes a witness to what we believe. The people had fallen a long way from what was fashioned with their own hands. And when we fall from the heights of our best moments, when we fail severely in surprising ways, the work of our better days cries out in objection. So the stones cry out, calling the people to return to their earlier intentions. Try not to be so hardened that you can no longer hear the stones.

Making The Most of Holy Week

The vibrant green of the palm branches on Palm Sunday, coupled with flowers and sweets of Easter help to lift us out of the winter doldrums.

That's not the whole story, though. Jesus walked from the peak of Palm Sunday down into the valley of pain and suffering in order to win the triumph of the resurrection. It is important to remember that Jesus suffered and died so that we would not have to. But I never want to get too far away for the price Jesus paid for my liberation. The eight days begun on Palm Sunday and concluded with Easter offer a chance to look into the abyss of a God-forsaken world, and to discover in the darkness the light of God's searching love. Make plans now to celebrate all of the events of Holy Week.

It I? Mark 14:18

Each friend of Jesus faced the question, "What kind of a person am I?" on this Thursday night a couple of thousand years ago when he blurted out, just right there at dinner, "One of you is going to betray me."

That wouldn't be me, would it?

LAUNCH

A new journey is launched the moment I can ask if I am the one betraying Jesus. Sure, I am capable of it, but that is not the question. And of course I wouldn't betray Jesus if I knew with certainty who he is, and what he came for, and what he is doing in the world, and how much he loves me, and how wonderful his plans for me are, and . . .

Is it I?

Questions for Reflection

Read Luke 22:14-20

What is the significance of the Last Supper taking place as a celebration of Passover (read Exodus 12:17-28 for ideas).

Why did Jesus "eagerly desire" to share this meal with his friends?

What does it mean for the Passover to find its fulfillment in the kingdom of God?

Launching in Lent

Is communion just something you do because everyone else is doing it? Or does it mean something more for you? What is that "something more?"

How does celebrating communion strengthen you to keep going with your spiritual practice?

11

Easter And Beyond

"Why are you looking for the living among the dead?"
    Luke 24:5

Easter And Beyond

The greatest moment of our faith is a moment of no faith. No one's head popped off the pillow on that morning so many years ago and thought, "We had better go to the burial area because we are likely to find Jesus alive and walking around."

Everyone confronted by Jesus that morning was a person of no faith. Everyone who heard the news was in a state of doubting when they began to believe.

Most people who have some faith still walk around carrying a great deal of doubt with them at the same time. This question, *Why are you looking for the living among the dead?* is a breakthrough question. It names a faith I don't yet have while neutralizing the doubts I swim in like a fish in water. I am looking for Jesus, and he is alive. So what am I doing among the tombs?

Those questions that launch a spiritual journey carry a living inkling of the way things were meant to be. Easter offers this transformative way

The Plan

Now that Easter is over you may be a little weary from all of the extra events and you may be experiencing some kind of settling in to the old routine. But Lent is preparation so that you are ready for Easter to launch you into new paths, deeper spirituality, or a greater sense of service. Consider what it will take to seal your resolve to live in the power of the resurrection.

of seeing everything. I only wish I could spend more time on the faith side, expecting to find Jesus alive when I come around the corner and enter any place that feels like death.

What is possible now?

On March 28, 1990, Michael Jordan, one of the greatest basketball players of all time, had the greatest scoring success of his career. He scored 69 points all by himself against the Cleveland Cavaliers. I haven't checked but I would guess that entire teams have scored fewer than 69 points in a game, and I wouldn't be surprised if at least once a team has won the game with 69 points.

After the game one of Michael Jordan's teammates was interviewed about the game. Stacey King was in his rookie season and managed to score two points in the effort. He humorously said, "I will always remember this game as the night Michael and I combined for 71 points."

And so I ask you, what can you and God accomplish as you team up together this year? When Jesus fed five thousand, as reported in Mark chapter 6, he didn't perform the miracle of creating a banquet for the great crowd of people out of thin air. Instead he used the five loaves and two fish offered to him by a boy. He multiplied the small gift and made it into something extraordinary.

... what can you and God accomplish as you team up together this year?

Challenges that seem overwhelming actually are. There are impossible things that need to get done and, no, you can't do them. When faced with an impossible challenge, the first step of wisdom is giving up. But only if followed by the second and third steps which are asking God for help and committing yourself to working toward God's miraculous and overwhelming triumph.

Faced with a habitual sin that you can't overcome? Give up, pray that God would do what you cannot do, and ask God to show you the way to freedom. Faced with a job that is above your skill? Give up, pray that God would do what you cannot do, and open your eyes to God's way of accomplishing the goal.

Those who regularly hear me pray notice how I struggle with this in prayer. I want to believe that praying is the most important solution to any problem, the most effective ingredient in any healing. But I forget what I sometimes have believed.

Let's commit ourselves, in the unknown year ahead, to believe that God is combining his score with ours for awesome victory. Let's help each other persevere in living by faith.

Questions for Reflection

Read Hebrews 7:22-25

Verse 22 has several strong words: oath, guarantee, better covenant. What message is the writer of Hebrews conveying with this choice of words?

What does it mean for you that Jesus is currently alive and interceding for you?

LAUNCH

Launching In The Power of The Resurrection

Will you go where God sends you?

Can you sense a calling that comes from somewhere beyond your own voice? In the quiet, when no one is around, do you understand that God has something for you to do?

Where do you see evidence in your own life of the power of the resurrection changing you?

12
A Word After Launch

. . . I press on toward the goal to win the prize for which God has called me heavenward in Christ Jesus.
>Philippians 3:14

A Word After Launch

Last year I got sick on Ash Wednesday. I was down for 8 days. That meant I had to miss the Ash Wednesday service and the First Sunday in Lent. All this in the year that I had launched this guide in my congregation.

I want to thank my wife, Annie, for stepping in at the last moment and leading the congregation through the Ash Wednesday service on just a few minutes of notice, *and* then turning around and preaching for three services on the First Sunday Lent. She is Co-Pastor with me on our staff. My sickness meant that while I was moaning on the couch, she was gracefully fulfilling God's call to lead in the unexpected circumstance.

This had not been my plan for how I would engage in Lent. Nor was it Annie's plan for how her Lent observance would begin. But Lent is all about what happens in the mix of our intentions and God's providence in circumstances.

You may have started the season of Lent with a plan, and you may have carried that plan to completion. Or events may have changed your plans multiple times. But now that it is over, what will you do to keep your momentum going?

Things don't generally remain fresh, pristine, and vital all by themselves. Roads develop potholes. Bread goes stale. The sink fills up with dishes. Paint fades.

And the passion of your faith is always growing dimmer. It is a reality of human nature. Just as waves can't always go up on the beach, they have to go back out again, so also it seems to be a

LAUNCH

spiritual law that the energy of faith advances and then recedes. These rhythms affect all aspects of our relationship with God: how we feel, how much energy we have for spiritual growth, and our capacity to serve.

This downdraft against our upward flight, this resistance to growth and thriving may be natural, but it is not necessary. If I can sum up what I meant to be saying with this book, it is an invitation to an ever-rising faith in a world that is sinking and threatening to drag us under with its pull.

While it is often valuable to relax and float down the river of God's love, spiritual growth advances through seasons of renewed attention to the next step. As C.S. Lewis described the progress towards Aslan's country in *The Last Battle*, we need to go "further up and further in." Maturity and depth—these are qualities often praised but attained far less frequently. Now that you have come through a period of growth, how will you take steps to keep it going? If you addressed chronic anxiety during Lent this year, what will need to happen over the next several months to make anxiety fade on a more permanent basis?

Further up and further in describes the life I want to live in this world, in preparation for the next. While savoring good things and anticipating a time when they will be more vivid might seem like a more fitting activity for preparing to be amazed by the wonders God has in store for us, I am convinced the counterpoint is equally part of the preparation. Refraining from rich foods, curtailing some activities, or adding practices to spur spiritual growth are all part of becoming more able to rejoice in the goodness of God.

So what are you going to do to keep going further up and further in?

I feel in some ways like I have been with you as you have launched your boat this Lent. I wish I could stay with you and discover how the next chapters of your life are unfolding but this is one drawback of writing a book. We are not together to turn this into a continuing conversation. Still I pray and hope you will avoid extended stays in the harbor and continue to thrive on the waters of God's great adventure.

In gratitude

As I mentioned in the last chapter, this book originally was printed in a shorter form as a guide for the season of Lent at Chapel By The Lake in Juneau, Alaska. I am so grateful to all of the members and friends of that church who gave me encouragement throughout Lent during the 2019 season. It was your response that led me to expand these pages and make them available to a wider audience.

I am thankful for all of my family members who gave me feedback as I was developing this study and encouraged me to continue. I am especially grateful for the encouragement of my parents, John and Martha Zimmerman. Each of you, in your own way, knew what to say to keep me going. Thank you.

www.ingramcontent.com/pod-product-compliance
Lightning Source LLC
Chambersburg PA
CBHW051406290426
44108CB00015B/2174